# Everyone Counts

## A Citizen's Number Book

Written by Elissa Grodin and Illustrated by Victor Juhasz

Sleeping Bear Press gratefully acknowledges and wishes to thank Professor
Michael Schudson (Department of Communication, University of California,
San Diego) and Thomas Collier (retired lecturer in history, University of
Michigan) for reading and reviewing the manuscript.

Sleeping Bear Press™
310 North Main Street, Suite 300
Chelsea, MI 48118
www.sleepingbearpress.com

THOMSON
✦
GALE

© 2006 Thomson Gale, a part of the Thomson Corporation.

Thomson, Star Logo and Sleeping Bear Press are trademarks
and Gale is a registered trademark used herein under license.

Printed and bound in Canada.

*First Edition*

10 9 8 7 6 5 4 3 2 1

Library of Congress Cataloging-in-Publication Data

Grodin, Elissa, 1954-
Everyone counts : a citizen's number book / written by Elissa Grodin;
illustrated by Victor Juhasz.
p. cm.
Summary: "Helps young readers better understand and appreciate their roles
as citizens of our country. Using numbers, this book takes readers on a tour
through America's system of government. Starting with the Constitution to
amendments passed thus far (27), to the number of senators in the Senate
(100), the parties, processes, people and history of our government are
explained"—Provided by publisher.
ISBN 1-58536-295-6
1. Citizenship—United States—Juvenile literature. 2. United States—Politics
and government—Juvenile literature. I. Juhasz, Victor, ill. II. Title.

JK1759.G76 2006
320.973—dc22                    2006015312

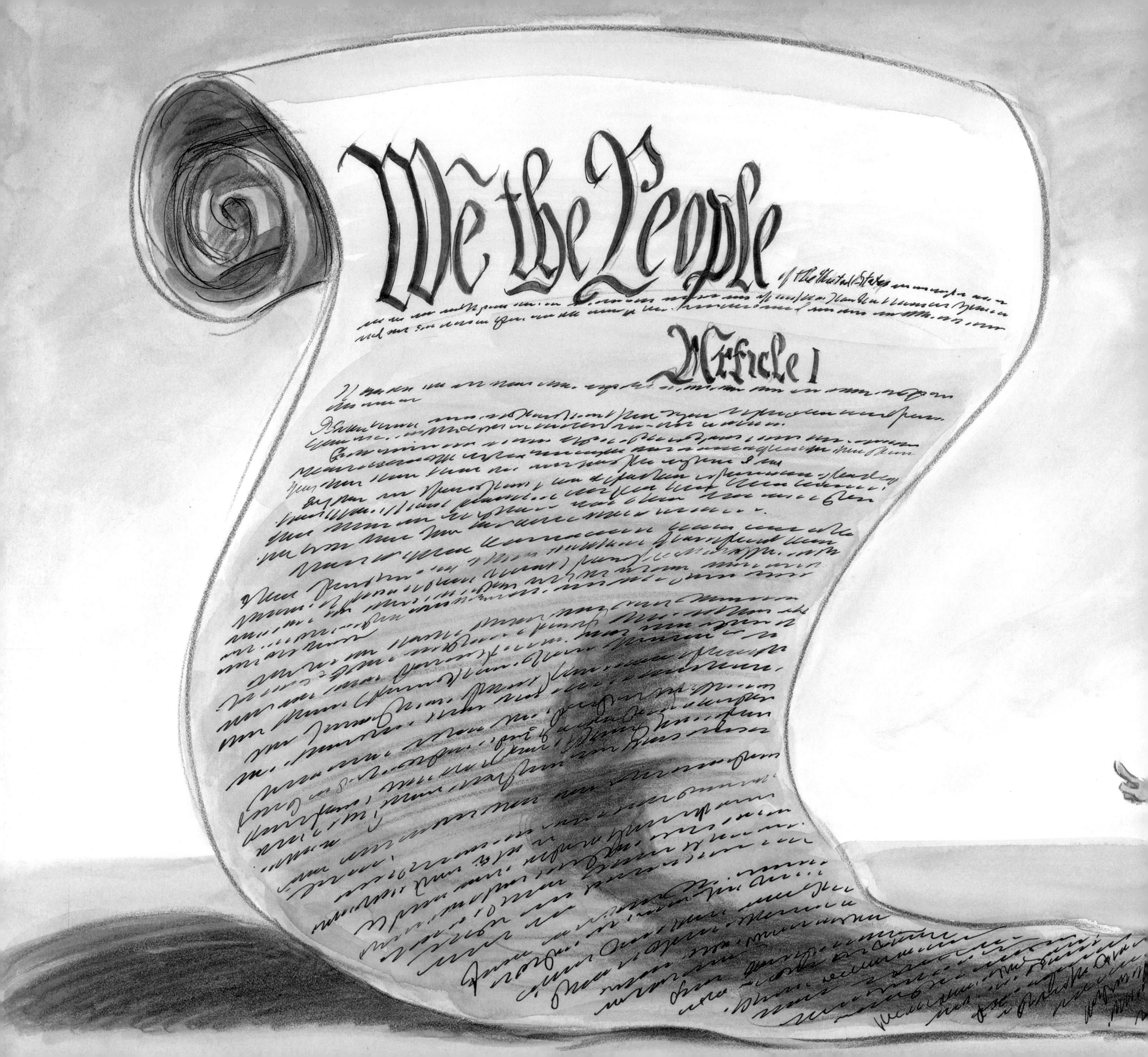
We the People
Article I

The battle for independence began
with a cry from every steeple,
and ended with 1 document
that started, "We the People."

Have you ever wondered what is so important about the United States Constitution?

In its early days America was a group of English colonies settled by people who, frustrated by a lack of freedom, left England. But even here these people still had to obey the laws of the English king. So in their desire for economic and religious freedom, they decided to fight a war against England to win their independence.

After winning the Revolutionary War, the colonies were free from England. But now what? America needed a form of government to run its new country. The brains of this operation were a group of men we now call the Founding Fathers. They wanted a government that gave people the kind of freedom they hadn't had before, the kind where everyone counts. Their design for a democratic government gave the political power to the people.

Starting with the words "We the People," the Founding Fathers hammered out the details of this new government in a document called the U.S. Constitution. All four pages of our Constitution are preserved and displayed in the rotunda at the National Archives in Washington, D.C.

one

1

Washington didn't want them
but because there was a fight
between Jefferson and Hamilton,
2 parties seemed all right.

A political party is a group of people who share similar ideas and philosophies about government. Here is a question for you:

Do you think the government should ban unnutritious foods so people don't become overweight or sick? Or do you think food companies should have the freedom to decide what kind of food to sell? This is a political question because it is about who should have the power to make decisions, and politics is about the distribution of power. Political parties have different views on this subject.

When the Founding Fathers were deciding how national elections should take place, there were no political parties. Alexander Hamilton and Thomas Jefferson were the two titans in George Washington's administration. Each a brilliant thinker, the two men disagreed somewhat with one another's political ideas. They had quite a feud going, and eventually two political parties arose from their differing views.

The Federalists, led by Hamilton and John Adams in 1792, were the first political party in America. In 1796 the Democratic-Republicans formed a party. This two-party system went through many changes over the years and has evolved into today's Democrats and Republicans.

two

2

**3** branches of government
separate all the power
so no one can get greedy
and democracy can flower.

EXECUTIVE

JUDICIAL

LEGISLATIVE

The GOVERNMENT

The Constitution's framers understood how important it was that no one individual would be able to get too much power. They wanted America's new government to be a democracy for the people, not a monarchy, where the king or queen makes all the laws.

They came up with a brilliant idea to ensure the safeguard of separation of powers. Three branches of government were fashioned which divided up the power. Each branch had powers that could act as checks on the other branches. This created a balanced form of government.

The executive branch makes sure that the Constitution is being followed. The president is head of this branch. The Congress, made up of the House of Representatives and the Senate, makes the laws. That is the legislative branch. The president takes care that the laws are obeyed. The Supreme Court is the guardian of the Constitution and makes sure all laws are in keeping with the Constitution. That is the judicial branch.

three

3

The Constitution states that the president should serve a term of four years. After that he may run for reelection as many times as he wishes.

George Washington became the first president in 1789. When America won the Revolutionary War, Washington was everyone's first choice to become the new president. He was a much-loved war hero and a great leader. President Washington served two terms and happily retired to his beloved farm.

The 32nd president, Franklin Delano Roosevelt (1882-1945), was so popular he was elected to four terms as president. People thought that was too much for any president, so an amendment (change) to the Constitution was passed. The 22nd Amendment (1951) limits a president to two terms in office.

Presidential elections get a lot of attention. A president is elected every four years, on the first Tuesday after the first Monday in November. Each political party holds a national convention before then to nominate its candidate for the presidential election in November.

four

4

It was time to choose a leader
and the country was excited.
4 years for George Washington
was unanimously decided.

Long before European settlers established themselves in America in the 1600s, a group of North American Indians had successfully set up a political union of their own. Five Indian nations had joined together so they might act as one. Have you ever heard the expression 'strength in numbers'?

In the late 1500s the Mohawk leader Hiawatha, along with his friend, Degan-awida, founded the Iroquois Confederacy. The Mohawks, Senecas, Onondagas, Oneidas, and Cayugas united in order to promote peace among themselves. This confederacy became a powerful political organization in America's early days.

five
5

The leader of the Mohawks issued a decree that **5** would band together to form a confederacy.

The moment America won the War of Independence against England, committees formed to come up with a design for an official United States seal. The idea was to create an emblem that proudly represented the beliefs and hopes of this newly independent nation.

The Great Seal was worked on for six years. The final version was approved by Congress on June 20, 1782. On the front of the seal is the coat of arms of the United States. It is full of interesting symbols, each with a special meaning. The American bald eagle represents strength, courage, and freedom. (In this case bald doesn't mean 'no feathers.' It comes from an old word 'piebald,' which means 'marked with white.') The Latin motto *E Pluribus Unum* means "Out of Many, One." Items numbering 13 appear over and over, including the stripes on the shield which represent the original 13 colonies.

You can see the Great Seal on the back of a $1 bill. George Washington is on the front.

six
6

**6** long years of planning in order to decide on an emblem for America to inspire a sense of pride.

New laws are passed by Congress but where do ideas for new laws come from? Remember the phrase "We the People"? Many changes start at the grassroots level by ordinary we-the-people like you and me.

Jane Addams (1860-1935) was an activist for social change and worked hard to improve life for others. In 1889 she started a neighborhood center, Hull-House, in Chicago where poor people and people new to America who did not speak English could come and study. Jane Addams organized members of her community to put pressure on law-makers. In this way, she helped get laws changed so that women and children who worked would have better protection in their workplaces. In 1931 Jane Addams became the first American woman to receive the Nobel Peace Prize.

Young people, too, have made meaningful contributions to American society. When Jennie Curtis (Chicago, Illinois) had to go to work as a teenager, she experienced unfair working conditions at the Pullman Train Company. Even though it meant she might lose her job, Jennie fought for better working conditions, and in 1893 she became the leader of the Girls Union of Workers.

seven
7

**7** grassroots organizers
work to make things better.
The only qualification
is to be a true go-getter.

The rules of citizenship
are important for all to know,
including **8** new people
who arrived not long ago.

Immigration is when people come to live in one country from another. Settled by people from all over the world, America is a nation of immigrants.

There are two ways to become an American citizen—by birth or by what is called naturalization. If you are born in America or born to American parents, you are automatically a U.S. citizen. If you immigrate to the U.S., you may become a "naturalized" citizen. Immigrants are allowed to become naturalized citizens if they meet the following conditions: They must be at least 18 years old, have a visa and a permanent place to live, and be able to speak and write English. After living in the U.S. five years, they must pass a citizenship test and take the Oath of Allegiance to the United States of America.

All citizens (born in America or naturalized) enjoy equal protection under the Constitution. In return, all citizens are required to:

- Perform jury duty, if called
- Support the Constitution & obey all laws
- Respect rights of others
- Pay all taxes
- Bear arms or perform other services for the United States when required

eight
8

CARDOZO    O'CONNOR    HUGHES    BRANDEIS

The Supreme Court is the highest court in the land. As the guardian of the Constitution, its job is to make sure that laws are in keeping with the Constitution. Here is one example:

In 1965 15-year-old John Tinker and his 13-year-old sister, Mary Beth, wore black armbands to school in Des Moines, Iowa, as an expression of protest against the Vietnam War. They were suspended from school for it. The Tinker family disagreed with this decision and took the school to court. The lower courts agreed with the school's decision, but the Tinkers kept appealing (disagreeing). The case went all the way up to the Supreme Court. The Tinkers won. The Supreme Court said John and Mary Beth had a constitutional right to wear an armband in school, and that the school did not have the right to suspend them for it.

History was made in 1981 when Sandra Day O'Connor became the first female justice appointed to the United States Supreme Court. Justice O'Connor retired in 2006.

*Justitia Omnibus*
Latin, for "justice for all."
Practiced by **9** members
sitting proud and tall.

nine
**9**

With **10** amendments added
there's no need to suppress
the thoughts and words protected
by freedom of the press.

The U.S. Constitution, a document of political, legal, and philosophical genius, wasn't perfect. In the beginning, several of the original 13 states refused to approve the new constitution because they worried it gave too much power to the federal government over peoples' individual rights. They wanted some amendments to be added.

James Madison (1751-1836) took the lead putting together a list of amendments. Out of the 12 that were proposed, 10 were ratified (made official) on December 15, 1791. These 10 amendments are called the Bill of Rights. They guarantee personal liberties such as freedom of speech, freedom of the press, and freedom of religion. Try to imagine what life might be like without them.

In the legal case *Board of Education v. Pico* (1982), Steven Pico took his school to court for removing nine books from the school library. School officials disagreed with some of the ideas in the books, and didn't want students to read them. The case went all the way to the Supreme Court, where it was ruled that the removal of books disobeyed the Constitution and ignored the students' First Amendment rights. Steven Pico won the case.

ten
**10**

**11** billion dollars
printed in new bills,
and a few billion more than that
filling up the tills.

This sounds like a lot of money but the United States Treasury Department prints much more than that each year: $82 billion! Most of the new bills replace old ones. A $1 bill, for example, has an average lifetime of only 17 months before it becomes too worn-out for use.

Every seven to ten years the designs on paper money are modified (changed), including adding colors. The formulas for the paper and ink used are kept secret. This is to help prevent the manufacture of counterfeit (fake) money. Even when newly designed money comes out, the old bills still keep their value.

In colonial times people used all sorts of things for money. Before the American Revolution, colonists used English, Dutch, Spanish, and French coins to buy goods. Sometimes they also used Native American beads, tobacco, and animal skins to do business.

eleven
11

A Constitution would replace
the Articles of Confederation.
**12** states would grant more power
to the new American nation.

Pennsylvania

Maryland

VIRGINIA

N. CAROLINA

S. CAROLINA

GEORGIA

DE

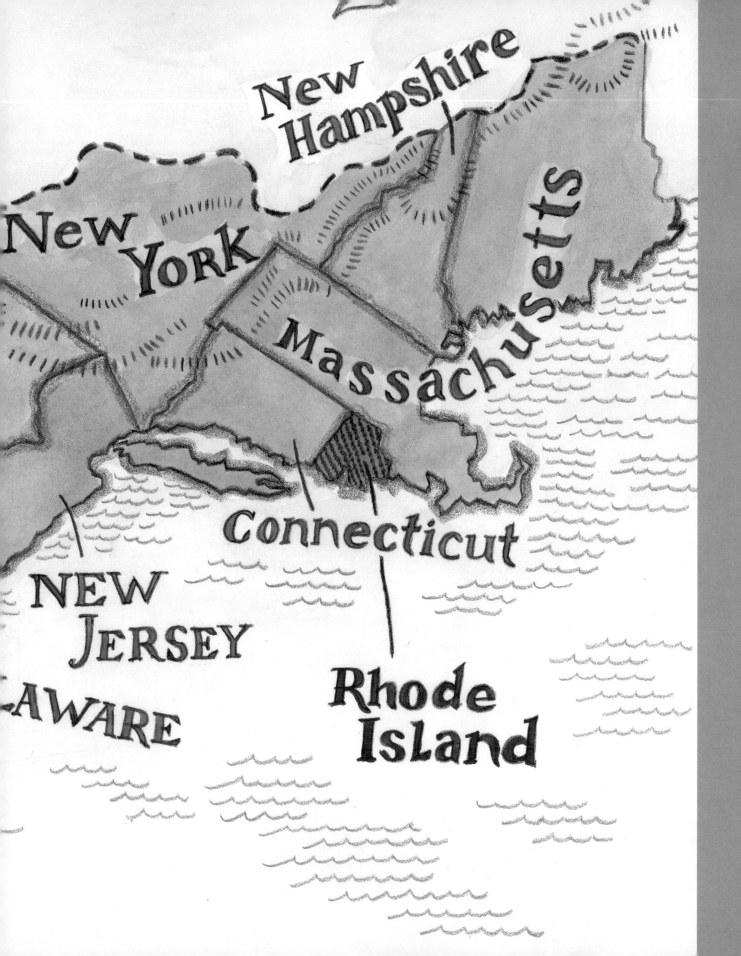

Thirteen American colonies fought in the American Revolution (1775-1783). When America won the war the colonies became states. At that time the states were governed by a document called the Articles of Confederation. Under this system, state governments had most of the power.

A Constitutional Convention was called in order to come up with a plan for a national government, which would be much stronger than the old system. In 1787 delegates from 12 states (Rhode Island declined) met in Philadelphia. George Washington was unanimously elected by 55 delegates to be in charge of the convention, which was held in secret and lasted several months.

Because of their vast knowledge of history, philosophy, and law, the Founding Fathers were able to write our Constitution, which is one of the most influential and important documents in history.

twelve
12

Good advice is crucial
**15** from people you can trust.
cabinet members
are a presidential must.

The cabinet is a group of people who head various government departments. At the beginning of a new term, the president gets to choose his cabinet members. They are usually experts in their fields, and often they are personal or political friends of the president. In the spirit of checks and balances, the president's choices must be approved by the Senate.

The oldest cabinet department is the Department of State. The members of the State Department travel around the world, promoting human rights and trying to help resolve conflicts.

The cabinet system is not specifically outlined in the Constitution. It originated in Great Britain, and in America it goes all the way back to George Washington, whose cabinet had four departments in 1789: State, Treasury, War, and Office of the Attorney General (the Justice Department).

Departments have been added over the years as America's needs grew. Other departments include transportation, energy, education, labor, agriculture, and others.

fifteen
15

Amazing as it seems, the framers of the Constitution figured out how this document would be able to keep up with the changing times young America would surely go through in the years to come. By allowing for amendments, the Constitution can adapt itself as society changes. Amendments are additions or changes. It is extremely difficult to get an amendment passed, however. Since 1791 only *27* out of over 10,000 amendments have been added to the Constitution. Remember what the first 10 are called?

Below are examples of how changes in our society brought about changes in the law:

**Amendment Thirteen** (1865) made slavery illegal.
**Amendment Sixteen** (1913) established income tax.
**Amendment Nineteen** (1920) gave women the right to vote.
**Amendment Twenty-six** (1971) gave citizens 18 years or older the right to vote.

The Twenty-sixth Amendment was the quickest to pass, taking only 100 days to ratify. The longest, Amendment Twenty-seven, took 74,093 days to pass! First proposed in 1789 and meant to be part of the original Bill of Rights, this amendment, which regulates Congressional pay raises, was finally ratified in 1992.

twenty

20

AMENDMENTS TO THE CONSTITUTION
① FREEDOM OF RELIGION, PRESS, SPEECH, etc.
② RIGHT TO BEAR ARMS
③ PROTECTS CITIZENS FROM HOUSING SOLDIERS
④ SEARCH AND SEIZURE
⑤ RIGHTS OF A CRIMINAL DEFENDENT
⑥ RIGHT TO A SPEEDY TRIAL AND CONFRONT WITNESSES
⑦ TRIAL BY JURY IN CIVIL CASES
⑧ NO CRUEL AND UNUSUAL PUNISHMENT
⑨ PEOPLE MAY HAVE OTHER RIGHTS EVEN IF NOT LISTED
⑩ POWERS OF THE STATES AND PEOPLE

**20**-some amendments
were voted into law.
A changing Constitution
was something they foresaw.

11 JUDICIAL LIMITS
12 CHOOSING THE PRESIDENT AND VICE-PRESIDENT
13 NO SLAVERY
[redacted]4 CITIZENSHIP RIGHTS
1[redacted] CITIZENS OF ALL RACES CAN VOTE
16 INCOME TAX
17 SENATORS ELECTED BY POPULAR VOTE
18 LIQUOR ABOLISHED - PROHIBITION
[redacted] WOMEN'S RIGHT TO VOTE
2[redacted] PRESIDENTIAL, CONGRESSIONAL TERMS
GOVERNMENT

Mrs. Catt was an activist
who gladly helped when asked
to launch a new amendment,
and after **30** years it passed.

NO NATION CAN RISE
ABOVE THE LEVEL
OF ITS WOMANHOOD

NATIONAL AMERICAN
WOMEN'S SUFFRAGE MOVEMENT

We have talked about the fact that amendments are very difficult to get passed into law. The Nineteenth Amendment gave women the right to vote in 1920. It took 30 years to pass!

Carrie Chapman Catt (1859-1947) was a teacher and one of the first female school superintendents in America. She was a leader in the campaign for women's suffrage, meaning the battle for women's right to vote. Mrs. Catt was president of the National American Woman Suffrage Association from 1900 to 1904, and from 1915 to 1920, when the Nineteenth Amendment was passed.

Victory did not slow her down. Mrs. Catt went on to establish the League of Women Voters, which to this day educates citizens about important political issues and encourages people to vote intelligently.

thirty
30

Rachel Carson (1907-1964) was a marine biologist and writer. By combining her love of writing and her commitment to nature, she changed the world.

Rachel Carson was the first scientist to warn people about how pesticides and other toxic chemicals were killing animals and damaging the environment. The big chemical companies were so afraid of her, they tried telling people she was crazy. But the world recognized the importance of this courageous scientist's work, and people supported her.

Her book, *Silent Spring* (1962), helped millions of people understand for the first time that harmful chemicals were ruining nature and should be made illegal. Citizens became very worried about polluted water, air, and land, and started putting pressure on the government. Carson herself testified before Congress in 1963, calling for new policies and regulations. In 1970 the Environmental Protection Agency was established. Its mission is to protect human health and the environment.

forty
40

**40** fish looking nervous,
worried about pollution,
waiting for politicians
to come up with a solution.

**50** stars for 50 states—
   Thirteen stripes have meaning, too.
      As for the colors, they couldn't be other
       than the familiar sight of red, white, and blue.

The 50 stars on the U.S. flag represent the 50 states. The 13 stripes embody the original 13 colonies. In chronological order of joining the Union as states they are: Delaware, Pennsylvania, New Jersey, Georgia, Connecticut, Massachusetts, Maryland, South Carolina, New Hampshire, Virginia, New York, North Carolina, and Rhode Island, all between 1787 and 1790.

Not much is really known about the origin of the stars and stripes, except that the very first American flag in 1775 incorporated the British Union flag. Also known as the Continental flag, this first flag was chosen by George Washington to celebrate the creation of the Continental Army. No one particular person designed the U.S. flag. It evolved gradually over time. Originally each star and each stripe was meant to represent a state, but eventually it was decided to add only a star for each new state.

In addition to the national flag, each state has its own flag, as well as a state constitution, and its own state symbols. Every state has elected officials, such as governors, state senators, and state representatives.

fifty
**50**

**60** votes were taken
from varying points of views
on who should be in charge
and what title he should use.

After the American Revolutionary War was won, and before there was a national government in place, each state was more or less in charge of itself. This allowed for all sorts of chaos. For example, when Rhode Island decided to print a huge amount of money that was actually worthless, the whole national economy was put at risk.

Soon enough a Constitutional Convention was called. State delegates met in Philadelphia in 1787 to develop a plan for a strong federal government, so things like printing money would be regulated (have rules). The convention went on for months, with much debate and compromise. The question of what to call America's new leader was voted on 60 times alone! Should America have a king? A president? John Adams suggested the title "His Highness the President of the United States." What about the question of how the states could have equal representation in government, even though some were much bigger than others?

George Washington was chosen to preside over the convention. With great leadership and a keen sense of fairness, he maintained order amid argument and disagreement, and guided the convention to a successful outcome.

sixty
60

Many people who serve in the government at local, state, and national levels are elected. Citizens can express their opinions by using their right to vote. Not voting means letting someone else decide for you.

You must be 18 years old and a registered voter in order to vote. People of any age can volunteer to help on a political campaign, though. You must be 25 years old to become a representative, 30 years old to become a senator, and 35 years old to become president. As far as running for office . . .

Michael Sessions was motivated to run for mayor while still a high school student. Michael was very concerned about the job cutbacks, including his father's, in his town of Hillsdale, Michigan. Michael saved $700 from his summer job, ran for mayor in 2005, and won by *two* votes.

You see, every single vote really does count!

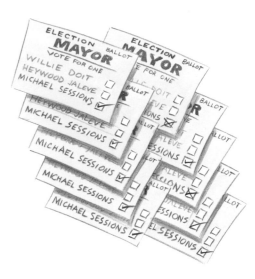

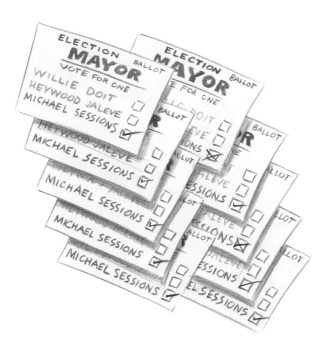

seventy

70

Ballots must be counted—
It's the democratic way!
just for starters
on a long election day.

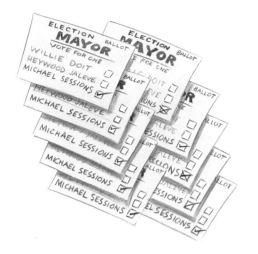

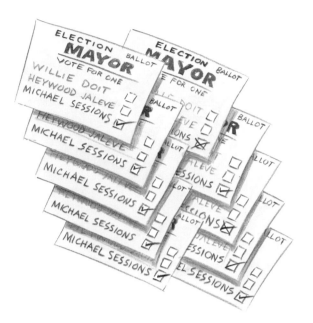

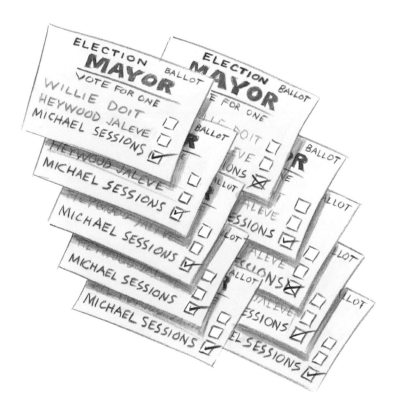

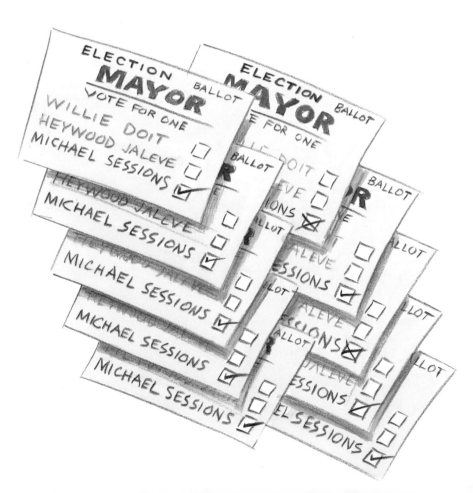

**80** fabulous roses
transmitting a heavenly scent—
Gardeners love to grow them,
including one president.

George Washington began planning for a garden at the White House by buying land from a tobacco planter named Davy Burns. That land is now the South Lawn of the White House. Washington was an enthusiastic gardener who loved to breed roses. How pleased he would have been that a couple of hundred years later, in 1986, the rose became our country's official flower.

Over the years presidents and First Ladies made many additions and changes to the White House gardens. In 1913 Ellen Wilson, the first wife of President Woodrow Wilson, put in a rose garden. Today's White House Rose Garden is on the same site and, located outside the Oval Office, has been used for many outdoor ceremonies including presidential speeches.

There are over 3,000 species of roses. The flower has been used throughout world history as a symbol of love, beauty, war, and politics. Given this illustrious history, it is easy to see why the rose was chosen as the official national flower of the United States.

eighty
80

An Englishman was greatly responsible for turning mass public opinion in America toward the cause of independence from England. While visiting England, Founding Father Benjamin Franklin (1706-1790) became friends with Thomas Paine (1737-1809). Paine wanted to travel to America. Franklin encouraged him and wrote letters of introduction so that his English friend would be well received when he got to America.

Tom Paine was a keen political writer and thinker. He wrote with great feeling about the revolutionary cause, and cheered America's desire for freedom. His famous pamphlet, *Common Sense* (1776), helped spur on the fight for independence. It was read by everyone in the Continental Congress, including George Washington. Its sales reached half a million copies at a time when the population of America was only about three million.

The power of the pen!

The Englishman Tom Paine
was an enthusiastic writer.
He turned **90** American readers
each into a fighter.

Congress, the legislative branch of the government, is divided into two chambers, the Senate and the House of Representatives. The Senate has 100 senators, two from each state.

When Senator Thaddeus Caraway of Arkansas died in 1931, his widow was appointed by the Arkansas governor to fill the vacant Senate seat. Hattie Wyatt Caraway became the first woman elected to the U.S. Senate when she ran to keep her seat in 1932. In 1841 Blanche Kelso Bruce was born a slave in Virginia. He eventually traveled north and went to college. After the Civil War Blanche Bruce became active in local politics. In 1874 Bruce was elected to the U.S. Senate as the first black person to serve a full term there.

People like Blanche Bruce, Rachel Carson, and Michael Sessions have something in common. They understood that circumstances can be changed by individuals who care. Rachel Carson's book made people aware of pollution in our environment and new laws were made to protect it. She and others looked at the world around them and worked to change things for the better. This is an opportunity every citizen has. Everyone *does* count!

one hundred 100

**100** senators in total
(two from every state),
working hard in Congress
with the House, to legislate.

## Elissa Grodin

Elissa Grodin attended Dartmouth College and the School of Visual Arts. She has written for the *Times Literary Supplement* and *New Statesman*. *Everyone Counts* is her fourth children's book with Sleeping Bear Press. She also wrote *D is for Democracy: A Citizen's Alphabet*; *N is for Nutmeg: A Connecticut Alphabet*; and the recently released retelling of Oscar Wilde's classic story *The Happy Prince*. Elissa lives in Wilton, Connecticut.

## Victor Juhasz

Victor Juhasz's artwork has been commissioned by major magazines, newspapers, advertising agencies, and book publishers, and his clients include *Time*, the *New Yorker*, *Rolling Stone*, the *New York Times*, the *Washington Post*, and Warner Books. He is a graduate of the Parsons School of Design.

Victor has three grown sons and currently lives in the New York Berkshires region with his wife, Terri. In addition to *Everyone Counts*, Victor's other books with Sleeping Bear Press are *D is for Democracy: A Citizen's Alphabet*; *R is for Rhyme: A Poetry Alphabet*; and *H is for Honor: A Military Family Alphabet*.